How To Talk To A Texan And Other Foreigners

Understanding Everyone - We're NOT All The Same!

Carolyn Franklin M. A.

voicedynamicscf@yahoo.com

ISBN: 9781091160811
Imprint: Independently published

Content

Years ago - and I mean *years* ago, I worked at hp when Dave and Bill used to walk by and borrow a screw driver for a minute. I worked in the Quality Control department, the only female.

Sometimes Dave would chat, but Bill never did. Maybe he was shy.

I tested voltmeters, ohm meters, frequency calibrators and oscillators. Do any of you know what those are? Hi tech! Seriously!

The engineers were mostly Americans at that time, but we did have a German, as I recall. Since Dave was a graduate of Stanford, almost everyone else was a Stanford graduate, too.

The "Q C" department was somewhat relaxed; the guys played jokes on one another, smoked cigars, put a lit cigarette under an instrument so smoke poured out and it appeared to be on fire, slipped a plastic worm into the supervisor's cup of coffee making him throw up.

The engineers knew cigar smoke made me sick to my stomach, so, for laughs, they'd deliberately blow cigar smoke around me. I got even by spraying a lavender air freshener around them. They complained! Said it smelled like a French whorehouse. The supervisor shrugged his shoulders - boys will be boys!

We got work done, too.

I was the only girl in the test department, but we had a real lady engineer - yup, Dave said so. On special occasions, like when De Gaulle visited us, Dave would take the Lady Engineer (as she was referred to) out of the store room and dust her off for exhibition. It wasn't like hp was in the dark ages!

She would stand between Dave and Bill with a glum expression. I think back now, seeing her there and I can feel her pain - a Barnum and Bailey exhibit! But, in those days, it paid well - for a girl, of that I was often reminded.

Actually I made .50 an hour and the engineers I worked beside got paid $1.25 an hour plus a share in the stocks. Girls didn't get shares. The girls on the line got .35 an hour and would shoot me dirty looks.

One day this tall, lanky Texan engineer ambled up to my work space.

"Y'wanna see m' noo nah?" He asked.

"Noo nah? … What's a noo nah?" I wondered.

Since I was bi-lingual, I already spoke Bostonian and Californian, naturally I was curious as to what a "noo nah" was - a new word in my collection.

"Sure."

He pulled out a bulging Swiss army knife, at least twelve blades, screw drivers, can openers, scissors, a saw, nail file, etc., their little sharp points sticking out as he slid them around like aces in Poker.

AHA!

NEW KNIFE! I had a new word - noo nah… new "knife"… in Texan! I filed it away in my "Probably will never come up again" file.

Then, much later, at vacation in Hawaii, I had a little motel room with a kitchenette. Early one Sunday morning - a knock on the door. I opened it.

A rather short, lumpy lady with frazzled, nondescript hair stood in the bright Hawaiian morning sun.

"Could Ah barrah a bowdah nah?" Were the inexplicable utterances from her lips.

A "bowdah nah….?" My mind went on hold. I stared blankly into the brilliant sun.

'Way back in the recesses of my mind I vaguely recalled hearing the word "nah" but couldn't link it to anything.

The woman stood there, un moving, perplexed, staring at me.

Finally, I brushed the cobwebs off the "Probably will never come up again" file, and up came the word, "knife!"

"KNIFE!! KNIFE!!!" I shrieked!

But, now, what was a "bowdah" knife…? BUTTER!! **BUTTER KNIFE!**

I was elated! "**YES!**" I shrieked - ran in the kitchen and got her a butter knife!

Clutching the prize, frowning, she turned and walked rapidly off into the blazing tropical dawn.

But, she spoke Texan, a whole new collection of odd sounds for me.

Let's move on to areas bigger than the Lone Star State to communicate with other foreigners.

Which brings us to now - smack dab in the middle of diversity - in America.

THERE WERE NO "IMMIGRANTS" IN AMERICA

At that time, I had already had 3 years of Spanish in high school, loved it. I also had 3 years of Latin. Loved it. And, I had a year of French. Loved it. But these were "foreign" languages.

For awhile the kids in my Spanish class went around saying, "Ola, John! Como se llama?" The response was, "Ola, me llama Roberto." But, that fad didn't last long.

That was the extent of diversity at that time, but we didn't know that word; we were just all Americans, some of who talked differently than others. No one I knew, except my family, all Italians, spoke a foreign language.

But, we were not "immigrants," my family came from Naples in 1898 to Fitchburg, Massachusetts. We all bought houses, had jobs and went to St. Anthony's on Sunday. We were New Englanders, or, as we prefer, "Yankees."

And, as Italians, we were quick to learn from the general public, all Italians were loud, ate garlic and drank "Daigo red." Oh, did they? We ate garlic, but I had no idea what "Daigo red" was. Pizza was not invented yet, but my grandmother made a flat bread with olive oil, garlic, tomatoes and anchovies, we called it "fugazza," the forerunner of pizza. I'd never heard of "pizza" - it wasn't from Naples.

There were no foreigners in America; we had no idea what an "immigrant" was - people in shawls off a boat? Oh, yes, we had

Irish people who celebrated Saint Patrick's Day. But that was only once a year. They weren't immigrants, they were Catholic. So were we. Italians and Irish were the same - Catholic.

Oh, well, then there were the Swedes who owned an apple orchard. And, uh, the Portuguese who had fishing boats and celebrated holy days with parades and hymns, and great cookies.

And then, Mrs. Stuart, who lived next door, made the best shortbread cookies. You should try them! She spoke Scottish, it sounded like funny English, actually quite musical.

Then we had some Mexicans who ate beans a lot and other stuff which was so good. I had something called a "taco" - the best thing I ever ate. I had two.

And there was a Chinese restaurant where they served some great food and some people ate with "chopsticks," but they were all Americans.

Oh, yes, there was China Town up in San Francisco. I assumed those were all Chinese people to keep the tourists happy and also were very colorful for us, the general Bay Area. To me it was sort of like a movie set. I loved going there, great food, hand-painted silk umbrellas, magic boxes for your secret things and little, tiny wicker doll furniture.

We had no foreigners in America, no immigrants; just Americans.

"Immigrants" and "Foreigners"

Then, I started college, San Francisco State College, a small school, in the 70's. I worked in the computer center recording student's names for Admissions.

I was at the key-punch machine; the next kid in line walked up to me.

I said, "May I have your name please?"

"You."

"No, not me, you."

"You."

Annoyed, I said, "No! Not me! What is *your* name!"

Also annoyed, he said, "My name is 'YU!'"

So I met my first foreigner, an immigrant...? He probably thought, "I just met my first American!"

Suddenly foreigners were every where! Immigrants! So, That's an immigrant - foreigners!, I thought as I walked down the halls of San Francisco State. The new people, the immigrants, were Vietnamese - just a name to me, meant nothing.

And, just as suddenly, students began protesting, something about Viet Nam, not wanting to go there, not wanting to be drafted, only cripples and women left at school, burning flags, burning draft cards, setting other students' cars on fire, bombing students' lockers...

There are no "immigrants," they're "foreigners."

Many Americans somehow linked the advent of foreigners with the concept of war. The term, "Vietnamese," was synonymous with destruction, the destruction of civilization, the eventual destruction of the American way of life!

They were Communists!

Americans panicked! We took sides - you were "for" or "against" - *everything!* America is good; everyone else is bad. It was obvious! Soldiers coming home in pieces, helicopters rattling as they landed with coffins of dead Americans - OUR BOYS! killed in Viet Nam! News commentators, dead, dying, bombs, villages, North, South, the news said something about a 38th parallel, Congs, Ho Chi Min, Saigon, all bad - the news said so!

I recall on the news, a very solemn reporter announced, "We have crossed the 38th parallel." I thought, "Thank God!"

Now, I had no idea what a 38th parallel was, but if the Americans, the good guys, crossed it - it must be good. Little did we ever know we had no business at the 38th parallel or any other parallel in Viet Nam.

Not until years and years later did we Americans come to understand the hell we created for the Vietnamese people in trying to free them from Communism. We still don't know the true story why we were there, and probably never will.

Not only did we have war now, we had immigrants and, drugs. Stoned, blank-eyed, spaced-out students either mumbling "Socialism, man, Capitalism exploits the poor…" or "Rights, man, rights for the poor…" No facts, names, data or evidence was forthcoming as to how Capitalism exploited the poor, or how America was rotten. Students saying these things were less than credible in their present spaced-out condition. Their lack of coherence obliterated any intelligence.

Other students, consumed by a flaming self-righteous fire argued vociferously in class, America is rotten!! Down with Capitalism! (this they cried as they cashed Daddy's tuition checks.) We need Communism - the perfect government, everybody rich and happy, free medical care…yeah, man, Socialism, no war - just share everything … you're for, you're against…what? I was never sure what we were for or against.

I noticed that those students espousing Communism had nothing to lose, but everything to gain. They were the "unwashed" intelligentsia, walking around, morose expression, sprawled on cots, chairs - wherever there was free food and free lodging, they were there, vacuously espousing "free whatever for all."

One could not but help these "intelligentsia" never provided sustenance for anyone, just assumed what was available fell from the skies. They "took" freely, but never "gave" at all.

With the Left there was no discussion, only flaming rhetoric fanned by Daddy's support money and "psycho-delic" drugs. The Right was wrong and the Left was Right. No discussion was permitted against the Left. Who wants to hear what's Right?

The only time the psyco-delics stirred was to inhale, pass out or shout down any input from the Right.

It seems capitalism was bad, workers were oppressed, poor, down-trodden… It all made no sense to me. Everyone I looked at, except for the glassy-eyed students, seemed to be prospering. Even the glassy-eyed students were doing well; they always had cigarettes - they could smoke in class then.

What they did had no relationship to what they said - "Love, man; that's what the world needs, love, man." And then their eyes would roll up in their head and they were gone - off to socialism in the sky - a world where there is plenty of everything - for nothing.

Free pizza and cheap wine for all

It seems the government was rich enough to pay for everything. But where did the Government get all that money? No one ever asked.

They said the money came from the Capitalists. But, if there were no Capitalists, where did the money came from, I'd ask. They'd roll their eyes to the ceiling, "You just don't get it, man."

That was true.

> *One of my friends, a good looking kid from an affluent family, went out begging every weekend. He stood on a street corner or in a shop doorway asking for "help." On Mondays, in class, he would gleefully tell me he "made" enough money to last the whole week! This was his concept of socialism, how you take from the rich and give to the poor. The "rich" - working Americans, were a source of ridicule in the far Left.*

After classes the students would meet in one of the Victorian apartments for cheap pizza and cheaper wine, chianti and "Thunderbird" sweet, white wine. They took the largesse of the sympathetic public for granted. And, after gorging on cheap food, spent the rest of the evening throwing up in the porcelain chalice.

America was thrown off balance. The world had tipped on its axis. America had become schizophrenic - we were split between an empty world of drugged minds, people who contribute nothing to society and the sight of the body bags of Americans, who had contributed their lives, coming home to families.

Asians came by the thousands, immigrants, boat people, brides - all choosing America for sanctuary, safety. They landed in OZ and we Americans saw them as "different." They were short, didn't speak English.

How could we relate to them - except by smiles?

Americans reacted with astonishment - who were these people? How do you talk to them? How do you get along with them? Asians were an unknown factor in the American Way of Life.

Confusion reigned. Fear of the unknown permeated the news.

Not until years later did it occur to me how strong was the fear and confusion in the hearts of these foreigners. We were tall, self-assured, land of plenty, everyone had cars, charge cards, indoor plumbing, we left food on our plates, threw away half-eaten sandwiches...

We didn't talk to them they didn't speak English - and, besides, what did we have in common with them? What could we say?

We Americans had no idea of the world they escaped from, their beautiful homeland, a lush, tropical, magical world suddenly ripped apart by strange men with weapons blasting indiscriminate death.

Then, the far Left shoved us all aside and blared orders through a megaphone: Hear ye! Hear ye! All Americans MUST love these immigrants! We MUST welcome them in! We MUST treat them like family, we MUST kumbyah, we shall overcome - *we must*...the press made it sound like if we didn't assimilate these immigrants we'd be facing eternal damnation.

The words, "immigrant," "Vietnamese," were synonymous with "killing," "war," - "terror" - Uh, we were plain scared! Americans began to feel very insecure. Who were these people coming to *our* country who live in war! That's not the way Americans want to live! We were on guard.

If the press had backed off, let us meet and greet slower, perhaps Americans would not have been so afraid of these little, terrified new-comers to our land. The press hit us hard with the big MUST word. Had our introduction to each other been kinder by the press, we all would have been much more comfortable meeting "strangers."

Except for the mid-West, where everyone was white, a farmer, no divorce rate, everyone a Christian, Fourth of July, Thanksgiving, Christmas, people got *married* before they got pregnant! and didn't live on welfare, there were no "immigrants," there were only "new neighbors." New people were welcome - they'd blend in eventually - no hurry. There's some "new" neighbors already living here. Moved here in 1953, 25 years ago. Right friendly people.

But the far Left, using the press as a club, made it a huge problem. Before this influx of strangers Americans didn't know we had a problem. But now we were terrified of public censure if we didn't accept the new-comers; and so, of course, you have a huge segment of Americans who will be damned if they'll do what they're told - "You can't tell me what to do!" Until now, we had all agreed tacitly on the right thing to do - we all got along.

But now, we took sides: FOR, helpless, terrified displaced families, or AGAINST people who were the "enemy" just a few weeks ago, killed our boys...

The press created a huge, ugly mess for everyone - the press threatened us, spewed hate for anyone who didn't follow the party line. Newspapers flourished.

So, here we are, all Americans now, a half a century later, trying to repair the damage of a war we had no business in and being fearful of a war-torn people who came to America desperately needing our help in so many ways.

But, we're trying to learn, understand and assimilate the best we could, trying to overcome the fascist far left - a little slow, but trying.

The purpose of this book is to understand how, in America, we are *different*. The general American propaganda is that we are "all the same."

No, *we're not*. And we don' wanna be all the same! Neither do immigrants - go in their neighborhoods and see how they live. Their neighborhoods are reminders of "home," the home they left for sanctuary in another world.

For a viable society we need to take care of the vast majority of people's health and safety needs. We need laws that protect the vast body of population so everyone prospers and lives with neighbors in a constructive way.

There always will be clash between neighbors as we must to agree on how far we'll go with others' tradition, mores and perceptions of disparate life-styles.

For example, one family stoned their daughter to death in the back yard. She had committed some infraction of their life-rules.

That's not going to work in America.

Another example, in a grocery store on a main street in a busy town the owners were killing animals in the back of the store and throwing the guts in the gutter. Flies everywhere.

That's not going to work in America.

Another example, a popular coffee shop dumped its liquid garbage on the sidewalk to the side of the shop.

That's not going to work in America.

Assimilation is one thing, but accepting and sanctioning practices Americans consider as unacceptable will have to be addressed, post-haste!

I was in the library of a relatively small town in the Bay Area (California). I went in the Ladies' Room to use the facilities. In each stall where I started in, none of the toilets had been flushed. I was furious! The "ladies," who had previously been ensconced in the stalls, were at the mirror fixing their hair and lipstick. I stood at a stall door and bellered, "I don't know how you people use toilets in your lives, but in AMERICA we FLUSH them when we're done!" The women totally ignored me! A girl, about age 10, rushed up to the stall she had apparently used, ran in and flushed the toilet. I was pleased and proud of her.

Many mainstream Americans think if you chastise a "foreigner," correct their behavior in some way, you're a racist, an "ugly American." The great Middle Class with its facade of political correctness seems to feel that to explain a social more is a criticism, and "unfair" to newcomers.

This is absolute ignorance. The people coming here *want* to assimilate, they *want* to belong, fit in, and how can they know what to do if we don't tell them?

One place I worked, one of the women from another culture, when she used the Ladies' Room, would stand on the toilet seat, leaving black footprints.

Not acceptable.

I went to another woman from the same cultural background, who was born in America, explained the situation and asked her to speak to the new-comer.

She did.

The problem stopped and no one's feelings were hurt. We just need to quietly explain how a situation needs to be changed and it is easily resolved.

And, yes, "Americans do it toooooo..." (this phrase is usually sung in a sweet, chastising tune...) There are far too many Americans already violating the health laws and restrictions, city health codes and city regulations as it is. These are addressed as soon as possible. Sanitary conditions are of prime concern in this country since day one. Laws apply to us all.

BUT, when you immigrate to a country, *when you live in that country, when you become a citizen of that country, then you must follow the laws of that country. It's not the "old" country - it's a "new" country - MY country.*

> *One of my students wanted to give a presentation on customizing neighborhoods. As is the current "politically correct" orders are to do all we can to make immigrants comfortable, she wanted to have neighborhoods where Mexicans could speak Spanish, have fiestas, Mexican food - totally Mexican. I said, "Yes, wonderful. But, there already is a place where you can do that - it's called 'Mexico.'"*

She said nothing. And, there are many Americans retiring in Mexico, learning the language and assimilating the customs. They're very happy there.

LET ME INTRODUCE YOU TO "AMERICANS"

Changing habits, mores, ethics, ideals and social basics, such as: Food groups, medical care, physically touching someone and sanitation can be challenging for some traditionalists from other countries. To ease that transition, this book will give you clear, unexpurgated information about who Americans *really* are, and how we view newcomers into our world.

THE BASIC CATEGORIES OF AMERICANS

(the categories we don't admit to - because "we're all the same")

The Super Rich and the Very Poor

The two extremes, the SUPER RICH and the VERY POOR, have exactly the same life styes. They have no sense of time, no concept of money and generally have no respect other people's property and rights. If they violate someone's rights... what can you do to them? Put them in jail?

When I say they have "no concept of money," the SUPER RICH have so much they don't need to think about it. They just breeze through the day doing whatever in the moment touches their fancy.

The SUPER RICH have business connections to offset any inconvenience. They don't have "friends" they "know someone." The VERY POOR have no cash, no cares, no schedule, no connections - jail is a minor inconvenience - but often they do have friends there - cousins, primos.

Also in either case, the concept of manners varies. The SUPER RICH do what pleases them when it pleases them, and the VERY POOR do what pleases them when it pleases them. Either side has little, or no, need to impress others.

And, lest you think the SUPER RICH have no charity in their hearts - not so. Every few months they'll have a "gala," which means a lavish ball and banquet on proportions to impress a Roman Emperor. They wear clothes inversely priced to the amount of material used and smile a lot for the cameras. The "proceeds" go to the poor - on stage, in front of the cameras, they display a huge check, about 6' by 3' with the amount conspicuously displayed on it. So you know it's all honest and aboveboard.

If you want to see where the SUPER RICH live, you can't go there; they have electronic surveillance, guards and Dobermans to establish the degree of welcome.

And, as for where the VERY POOR live, you don't want to go there.

For the VERY POOR their conversations revolve around why there's no Mountain Dew in the 'fridg and did Emma Lou have her baby yit. Uncle Curley shot three deer last week upinna hills - missed a dam buck, gotta coupl'a squirrels. Their friends stopped by with an extra case of Mountain Dew to share.

If the VERY POOR live in the city their conversation revolves around where to get some pot, a roach, a joint, a hit…none of which they'll be able to spell as they text each other in their latest iPhones. Oh, yes, the super poor manage to have iPhones on their sparse income.

The Super Rich and Nouveau Riche

The SUPER RICH are divided into two classes: OLD MONEY and NOUVEAU RICHE.

Simply put, people of OLD MONEY are rarely seen. They drive very old cars, wear very old clothes, haggle incessantly over the price of a turnip, rarely pay bills (usually they have a lawyer to handle those crass details) and never carry cash - they expect you to pay. They do not have friends - they have rank.

They live in handsome mansions on acres of land hidden by a dense forest. The mansions are filled with portraits of people long gone and forgotten, but painted by Stuart, Bosch, Vermeer and others. They're rarely home - usually visiting a Count in old Rome. Their conversations revolve around where they spent last weekend and where they'll spend next weekend. They do have children but they're in a boarding school somewhere.

Examples of OLD MONEY are Queen Elizabeth and...uhmm...that's about it. She doesn't live here.

The NOUVEAU RICHE are people who became famous by popular demand: Sports figures, movie and TV stars, politicians and lottery winners. They have no taste, no ancestors, no class, no history - just a lot of diamonds, big, fast cars and a weirdly shaped swimming pool.

They live in vast, spread out, sprawling one-story homes with glass walls - the better for you to see their latest "collection" of Andy Warhol and Charles Schulz. They do not have friends, they have connections.

Examples of NOUVEAU RICHE are any woman who's been on TV wearing clothes that accentuates their Gluteus Maximus or their mammary glands. Men wear tight jeans, jackets, shirts with open collars.

THE AMERICAN MIDDLE CLASS

This group, also, is divided into two sections: UPPER MIDDLE CLASS AND LOWER MIDDLE CLASS.

The UPPER MIDDLE CLASS is extremely conscious of "things," those being: the latest and biggest car, the best University for their kids (usually 2 kids, possibly 3), the right ZIP code, a Mexican house-cleaner named Lupe and a gardener named Jesus. The home owners do not speak Spanish and Lupe and Jesus do not speak English. They all smile at each other a lot.

They have every piece of technology put out since last night and, know how to work them - even the kids do. The house is two-story, 5 bdrms, 3 1/2 bths, 5 car garage, pool and sauna. They have two Lhasa Apso's. They have installed the latest surveillance equipment and have a private guard to patrol the neighborhood.

If they see a neighbor outside the house, they nod at each other and smile. Perhaps once a year they have a neighborhood BBQ where they smile a lot and say things like, "we've got to help the poor, housing for the homeless, get kids off drugs, control guns, get the Democrats out of office, get the Republicans out of office, we need more public tennis courts, my church is having a fund raiser…" They usually have small hamburgers on dry buns and a beer or a glass of red wine.

They belong to a club of select members; they play golf, bridge, tennis, squash and go boating. The club has charity drives twice a year to help the needy. Their conversations are limited to: Their trip to Mazatlan where they saw some pyramids - really old ones, NASDAQ, DJ, losses, gains, investments, returns, market trends… They have standing appointments with their therapists.

They do not have friends - they know the "right people."

The LOWER MIDDLE CLASS owns all the same kinds of cars, well, almost. They're the step-down model of the expensive cars, bought on a 10 year loan but they'll up-grade just as soon as the husband gets a raise and his bonus. They belong to a church (Christian), the woman teaches Sunday school, they smile a lot and are benevolent.

They have three kids, but the middle one is having a setback; he's in detox. The congregation is praying for him.

They have a 4 bdrm 2 1/2 bth home, mortgage and second mortgage. The wife does all her own housework and is a mgr. spec. in IT. Her car is slightly older and will be paid for in two years. His car will be paid off in five years. They have health insurance, house insurance, insurance for two cars, dental bills, braces, the newest phones for each family member, cable, internet, several apps and the house bills as well as the vet for "Morki" and "Tina." Morki has seizures.

When the husband and wife have marital stress, the Pastor tells them God will provide. They have 6 credit cards, three maxed out. They have friends at church they enjoy and have BBQ's often. They talk about football and recipes. They are good neighbors.

After having said all that, there is no "class" in America! Just ask any Harvard student majoring in law.

And the sad thing is, we really believe we're "all the same."

We are *equal*, not the *same*.

We're just a little hypocritical in our perception of who counts and who we overlook in society. But if you should mention this obvious disparity in life styles and our vacuous deception, we'll vociferously deny differences - we're a "melting pot," a "daisy in a garden of flowers," a "bowl of vegetable stew" where we're all carrots and potatoes, a bowl of mixed nuts.

The challenge of interacting

Now that you have met the basic American, let's find out how he needs to interact with people of:

different social habits

different work ethics,

different communication styles

different religions

different hygiene practices

different languages

We're *equal* - we're not the *same*!

In my classes, as a Communication Studies Instructor, I had - literally - students from almost everywhere in the world, hundreds of them. Of course, in college, you have the top of any given society. Generally people of any culture send the best and brightest of them on to achieve knowledge and success (in their definition).

Because of the privilege of having a one-to-one interaction on a daily basis and in a rather intimate setting, a classroom, from my students I had the opportunity to discover perceptions, confusions, questions, digressions, habits, traditions - and more of the possible and probable clashes among cultures in their various ways of life.

As a personal note, I enjoy people from everywhere. They bring new ideas, fresh insights to a different way of life. We can see where we differ and where we share in Life's journey. It's broad horizon and a new world for us all.

EDWARD T. HALL HIGH AND LOW CONTEXT OF INTERCULTURAL COMMUNICATION

That is what I am now sharing with you, the many beliefs and distortions among the varied cultures in today's encapsulated, scrambled, mismatched, blended societies. And, I will base much of my conclusions on the basis of Edward T.Hall's High and Low Context of Intercultural Communication. This is the only Intercultural Theory that made any sense to me.

The population for Hall's study in 1976 was blue collar factory workers, all males. Over the passage of time the results of his theory today are somewhat modified. But, since habits, beliefs and norms are slow to change, the results of his research are still reasonably valid.

HIGH and LOW CONTEXT

Let's begin by defining terms. This is what I tell all my students, first explain what you'll be talking about. It's interesting how few people agree on terminology. So, you have to first establish what you consider the concepts to mean.

"Context"

The word, "context" means the "environment," the physical location where interaction takes place. Are you communicating camping in the mountains, slurping soup at the office cafeteria, sprawled on the couch in your living room or are you at the office conference room with all the big C's watching you?

At the time when Hall observed his population, America was a very different place. The general public had established ideas of who was who and how we were supposed to act within that confine. We all had a place and stayed there. The reality of distinctions had not surfaced; if you were born here, or moved (immigrated) here, you were American - period.

We were - really - all "the same" - then.

Not until the Far Left, the Progressives, controlled the press and told us we were all different and Americans should accept that difference - we should all understand we're the same because we're different. Therefore, we're all the same. To see "difference" is racism, prejudice, ignorance, hate mongers - *does this make any sense*!!

I found myself very confused. I shut down when faced with stupidity. Simply put, we should celebrate "difference;" accept it, learn from it - enjoy it!

In this case, by today's peripatetic population, we have found there are relatively few areas that are spared the looming golden arches of McDonald's - and, because of internet we now know more of who is who.

When your surroundings "talk" to you, say who you are, what you're doing, "speak" to others with no words, that is "high in context." At a funeral, you're sad, in tears, head held down, silent, that is "high" context. You need no words to understand; the surroundings, environment "speak" the content of the situation.

The surroundings, the context, are "high" in telling you what is happening.

High-Context Cultures

According to Hall, the countries of High-Context cultures include:

Asia

Mexico

Native Americans

African Americans

In the High-Context grouping Hall also includes Hispanics. These are cultures that use low, non verbal communication. They have strong traditions and habits so verbal communication is a low priority.

HIGH-CONTEXT GROUPS DEFINED

(Native) American Indians

American Indians are "high-context" groups, according to Hall. They're tribal. If you're born in a "nation" of people having certain religious observances, specific philosophies, child rearing practices and a history of heroes, you don't need words - you know who you are and what to expect.

American Indians as "Native" Americans:

Anyone born here is a "native" American. With my small part of Osage Indian I deeply resent being lumped in with Choctaw, Cherokee, Sioux and the many other Indian Nations under the White man's definition of my heritage.

I fully expect many other tribal people feel the same way. The various Nations of the American Indians have many, many different customs, religious observances and family structure. We are not a collection of tribes, each tribe is *its own nation*. Leave us alone!

It's kind of like saying, "'Thee' European lives in an old castle on a cliff and eats lots of cabbage and sausage. He plays a concertina and worships the rising sun in a circle of big stones.

We are not all the same! But we are all Americans!

(By the way, fellow Indians, Columbus did NOT discover America - let go of it.)

Mexicans

Mexicans never were "Hispanics." Yes, Spain landed ships full of conquerers in Mexico and Chinese merchants landed fleets of rice and silk (where do you think Spanish rice came from? - arroz con pollo…?). There was significant commerce between China and Mexico in the past 500 years or so.

And sailors, like sailors from everywhere for as long as there have been ships, co-mingled Chinese with the beautiful Mexican girls, giving rise to a new generation of blood types. Perhaps the Liberals should read more history and perhaps come up with the soubriquet for Mexicans as, "Hispanese"?

So, I do not see the natives of Mexico as high-context. I have found the women love to discuss recipes and children, as well as any culture, and the men discuss whatever men discuss…how hard work is, their boss is a jerk, the roof leaks…

In all my travels in this world, I have never met any people so ignorant of history and the various cultures as Americans - what we don't know, we make up. I ordered a pizza one place - in America, and the guy said did I want sausage or pepperoni? I patronizingly explained, "pepperoni IS sausage," where he became outraged at the thought it wasn't meat..(oh, god…)

So, if you are a new-comer to America, you'll probably do as well as anybody else.

> *I was in an Indian deli, the clerk was Indian and the customer was English. They both spoke British English but neither could understand the other. I was amazed. I translated for them; to me, they were both very clear. The clerk asked, "Can you understand him?" pointing to the Englishman. And the Englishman, in some astonishment,*

asked if I could understand the Indian. I still can't imagine what they didn't understand...

"African" Americans

"African" Americans is such a blatant misnomer - where to begin...? ALL the Blacks *born* in America, are Americans - NOT "Africans," NOT "African American." If they choose to have a specific common national appendage it should be clearer than that of "Africa."

There is NO *country* called "Africa." And, like American Indian tribes, Africa is composed of many countries with most of them having Black citizens, but also some Brown and White.

Africa is NOT united - it is a continent of specific cultures.

In my classes of students representing the world, The African students (the *real* ones), do not want to be "African" American - they are Congo , French Congo, Belgian Congo (Congan is not preferred), Kenyan, Sundanese, Eritrea... They do not want to be lumped in one ethnic lump. They have specific identities - just like American Indians.

I am amazed at how many Americans think Africa is a country. One friend, born and raised here, in his 70's, insisted Africa was somewhere near Saudi Arabia, around Egypt. He kept trying to show me where it was on a map, but we didn't have enough time to find it.

Pathetic.

In the Mid East, men "kiss" on greeting each other. But, they are not "kissing" in their culture; they are exchanging breath, the basis of Spirit, the essence of Life. To exchange "Life," is the greatest honor they can give someone.

They do not touch any woman except their wives and daughters.

And, being ignorant of geography, we want to control other countries' identities! (Arrogant?)

> *One of my friends in Sunnyvale, CA told me she would not be available for a meeting tomorrow, she was going to Pikes Peak. I was confused, Pikes Peak...tomorrow? Odd, she'd never mentioned that trip before... Perhaps it' s a pizza place nearby - like Mountain Joe's?... Two weeks later she called me, "Do you know where Pikes Peak is?" She demanded. "Uh, yes..." I replied. She went on to tell me how she drove for days, how far it was... I said nothing.*

Some High-Context Communication

If you're regularly communicating with others in the workplace office, not many words are required to explain why the desks and cubicles are placed where they are. You already know. You know how to act, how to behave in that context because you've done it many times. That is "high" context - lots of cues as to where you are, *no words* needed.

A classroom is the same, desks, chairs, windows, white board, teacher up front, students seated facing front - no one has to tell you this is a classroom - it is "high" in "context" - "low" in "words" - *no words* are needed.

According to Hall, in ancient countries, such as Japan and China, the customs and life-style are high-context. The people in Asian countries do the same actions century after century, same dress codes, same daily behavior patterns, specific rituals for death and marriage are observed. Work habits are strict and highly structured, as is education. These codes and rituals include *everyone*.

They're not loquacious - they don't talk a lot, explain actions, explain goals, because they don't need to. Everyone, more or less knows what's going on or what should be going on. What they do, they've always done; no need for words.

Since these people in Asia have lived the way they do for centuries, because of inter-breeding, to us, they look alike, think alike, act alike and have the same expectations and goals from century to century. Individualism is neither allowed nor understood.

Therefore, communication is a "given," no words are necessary - high context.

> *A Korean student took me out to lunch to a Korean restaurant. The waitress placed a square dish of food at my place. I started to eat and my student got annoyed. He said, "NO! You have to start at the upper right corner and eat each section clockwise!" So, of course I asked, "Why?" Annoyed still, he replied, "Because that's the way you eat your food!"*

So, to please my student, that's the way I ate my food! Odd, it tasted just like the food I ate haphazardly!

However, in this High Context grouping, Hall has included Hispanics, Native Americans and African Americans.

In this case, by today's peripatetic population, we have found there are relatively few areas that are spared the looming golden arches of McDonald's, and because of internet we now know more of who is who.

Asia is considered high context - and - in America we also have villages, hamlets and communities that are high in context. In the mid west and deep south, people live by tradition. Things are done one way, "it's done this way," and that's the way it's been done since 1492.

LOW-CONTEXT GROUPS DEFINED

According to Hall, some Low Context Cultures are:

America (North)

Australia

England

Germany

These countries are very similar in behavior, social interaction, mores, ethics and have common styles of communication. According to Hall, we are verbal, talk a lot - in the same language, explain a lot, require contracts to seal business deals, have similar table manners, marriage contracts and similar courts of justice.

And this is, basically, because we Americans are derivatives of England. The German language, in itself, may be different than English, but much of the German vocabulary is entrenched in English communication. English is also heavily influenced by Latin.

Americans and Australians speak English as their base communication language. We talk a lot, constantly questioning, explaining, probing, "How, why, when, how much, where…" Lots of words but not always much substance - in American.

So, why does Hall label us as "low context"?

Recently I was in the San Francisco DeYoung Museum of Art. It had been rebuilt to meet earth-quake standards and the concept of "museum" was completely overhauled. From the outside the museum looks like a "bunker" to hide in if there were an attack from the near-by Pacific. You walk in, and walk in, and walk in down a broad, interminable dark hallway that led to some dark area where I chose to avoid. As for art, the hallway had a Chihuly glass chandelier which, I supposed, some decorator had hung there and forgot about it. I left.

This museum, on the other hand, had no cues, no "words," nothing even remotely familiar in the sense of "museum." It was definitely "low" context in that environment. When measured against the common idea museum, there was no relationship - I needed *lots* of words to explain that dark "emptiness" I wandered in.

Communication usage varies

Communication in "Context" is the "language" *of the area* around the "talk."

For example, if you were at a birthday party holding a small, empty plate, it might mean you wanted a slice of cake. But if you were at a gift shop holding an empty plate it might mean you want to purchase it. And if you were at my house holding an empty plate, I'd put it in the dishwasher.

The area, the environment, the "context" surrounding the words, is the major part of the message you interpret.

Subsequently, over the years, I became a Communication Studies Instructor and had students from most parts of the world, even one or two from Texas. Some of my students were adept at languages and others had considerable trouble wrapping their tongue around the devilish, whimsical, English sounds.

Each student believed he or she was pronouncing the specific words correctly. Sometimes they hit the mark and some times far from it.

In my class they were required to give speeches, give oral critiques, and respond orally to discussions. When you consider stage fright was a decided factor in "public" speaking, not knowing enough vocabulary to speak at ease, and having to deal with the various dialects and eccentricities of Americans - the challenge for English-as-a-second language students could be overwhelming!

Much of the time no two Americans spoke the same "language." My work included interpreting concepts, and the students were always helpful getting us over cultural idiosyncrasies, odd "sounds" and definitions.

For example: In the southern states, the vowel sound "i" as in "like, "time," "nine," does not exist. They insert an "ah" sound, "lahk," "tahm," and "nahn."

All sounds are very soft.

> *I was dining with two friends from Arkansas. They said, "Let's have some pah." I assumed "pah"was an Indian dish as the deep south has much Indian influence. No, they wanted "pie."*

However, in the Florida panhandle, they speak a very strong "hillbilly" exactly like the "Beverly Hillbillies." At first I thought they were kidding me, but no, they really talk that way!! There's no way to - easily - record it in script.

Louisiana in some areas use a "patois," a sort of inside-out English heavily influenced by French. Very hard to understand, impossible to follow.

I already mentioned Vermont. Massachusetts has no "r" at the end of words, such as "car," "where," "sure," and so on. Try "cah," "wayah" and "shoo-ah."

In the mid-west, Oklahoma, Nebraska, Kansas, the people speak "farm" language comprised of idioms and colloquialisms. Too many to count. But, what you really need to know about the Mid West, farm country is, no one has names.

Each person is called, "Father," "Mother," "Sister," "Brother," according to the family relationship. No matter what area you're in, families will address each one, "Sister, go get Brother. Father wants to take your picture." "Brother, do you know where JJ is… Father wants JJ and JR to set with Sister and Mother at the table."

If there is more than one son, to differentiate on occasion, they'll use the initials of the first two names.

The selection of names is somewhat restricted for ease or tradition. Boys will be called: JR, being the first choice, JJ, JB, JD or J…

Girls are the same. Their names will most likely be: Bettyjane, Bettysue, Bettylee, Bettyann, Betty… or, Pattysue, Pattylee, Pattyjane, Patty… or, Marysue, Marylee, Maryann…

I did meet two sisters in Nebraska, tall and thin, similar faces, named: Bessiebelle and Clarabelle. I couldn't tell them apart.

In the wild West, the dialect is reasonably coherent and similar. Words are more easily recognized and spoken.

Intercultural caveats

Because it's so easy to misunderstand someone from a different culture, there are basic events to avoid at all costs. This precaution applies to everyone. The interpretation of words in business can be carried over from their meanings in disparate cultural interpretation.

1. *As a rule it's always best to get any financial agreements in writing with <u>anyone</u>. There can be misunderstandings; when two cultures collide the situation can get very unpleasant. It's so easy to misunderstand some agreement or concept and when there's language confusion there could easily be monetary loss, and there could be serious repercussions.*

   *Get any **agreements** of any consequence, in **writing, dated and signed.*** This way both sides are covered if there is a misunderstanding. And, you can clear up any problems before signing a contract.

   Caution: It is often the case, where, in high context cultures, they assume any arrangement is agreed upon by both parties by smiling. One side smiles and then it is assumed the deal is closed.

   No.

   Don't be deluded. In some cultures the smile is just that - a smile. No agreement has been reached. Americans will assume it is, but, no, no, no - it's not. *Get any critical agreements signed and dated by both, all, parties.*

   Do not depend on nods or assumptions - promises, no, no, no!

2. Keep your hands to yourself; don't pat, hug or stroke anyone other than your twin brother. In the Asian countries it's permissible for boys to hug boys and girls are very close, physically, to each other. They're like a family. But genders *do not touch each other.*

35

3. Honor anyone's "personal" distance. Try to stand at least 2 feet away from anyone if at all possible. Americans, in particular, do not like to be touched or have anyone stand close to them unless it's absolutely necessary. When someone is standing "in our space," we get very irritable - stand back! And, we do not share, necessarily. Unless pre-arranged, don't come into "my" space and *do not touch anything of mine* unless you get permission. An American is most uncomfortable in a crowded elevator. Sometime note how they stare at the passing floor numbers overhead. They don't want eye contact with anyone - that's too intimate. Islanders, like Asians, are communal; they stand close to each other and share what they have at the time.

4. Eye contact is critical, very Western. If you don't look into our eyes, we assume you're hiding something. An Asian is uncomfortable with prolonged, direct eye contact.

However, eye contact in *close physical quarters* for an American can be unnerving - too intimate. We prefer maintained eye contact at a distance of 5 feet or more acceptable.

And, I have found there are American Blacks who do not appreciate direct eye contact. I had one very close friend (Black) that I spent much time with. As we talked, I would look directly into his eyes and he'd look over my shoulder - drove me nuts.

I kept trying to move into his line of vision, insisting that he look directly into my eyes, but he was most uncomfortable. Finally he told me in his social situations looking directly in someone's eyes is a sign of aggression - you're challenging someone to a fight.

That was disappointing to learn, but certainly valuable information. I still looked in his eyes and he did try at least to maintain eye contact with me. I appreciated that.

INTERCULTURAL IDEOSYNCHRACIES

Communication comes in many forms, some of them verbal, others are a bit thin on meaning for the uninitiated. In recent years, often, when you ask someone a question, they just stand and stare - no verbal response. This blank look, lack of

"answer/response" is fairly new, and very annoying.

I personally suspect this lack of verbal interaction is the result of high tech - we use text, emojis, acronyms and to respond by looking over someone's head with a blank look implies a serious lack of intelligence. Not good.

Some types of communication, in general, are:

Non verbal, verbal, covert, metaphors, paralanguage, silence, accents, tears, laughter, cultural influence, staring and smiles.

The following categories are basic break-downs of basic communication styles.

"East" is Europe and all the countries east of Europe. "West" is all the countries west of Europe. This division is ancient and a cultural phenomenon.

NATIONALISM

Probably most readers of this book will have families that they love, support, cherish and enjoy. Probably some family members need help from time to time or even admonishments as to choosing a better path of life.

When you love and enjoy your family, does that mean that you have to exclude all the neighbors - you can't like any of them? Is there only room enough in your life, your heart for a specific number of people?

Of course not.

So it is with nationalism. It's *your* country, you should be proud of it. Nothing is perfect, but we can always do our best and improve as time moves along. There are those American citizens who feel nationalism is a type of racism, a type of capitalism or some kind of irrational support of their home country.

Yes, it is irrational, but on their part. Every country has some aspect that needs improvement. To see America as to blame for widespread global poverty and lack of political integrity is irrational - unintelligent.

THE THREE (3) MAJOR DIFFERENCES BETWEEN EAST AND WEST *TAKE THEM SERIOUSLY*

	East	**West**
TIME	Time is infinite	Time is finite
VERBAL	High context	Low context
	Low verbal	High verbal
PRONOUN	Communal **WE**	Individual **I**

Yes, take them seriously. Much of the time Americans protest that "we're all alike" - except for the differences which - we should just ignore.

It's not nice to be "different " -

But, we are.

And, it's ok. We don't have to be alike - but we do have to respect each other.

We begin with the Chinese culture to represent Asia in general.

CHINESE (Asian) Communication is contextual (low verbal)

Major pronoun is "we"; they're communal

China is vast; much of it is still open country. In centuries past, people lived in small farming communities - villages. Outside of marauding Mongols, Huns and sundry tribes, the Chinese had

39

little influence from the outside world. Their lives were predictable; their traditions are ancient and their family structure is solid.

In villages people know each other; each person knows the daily routine from birth - things just don't change much in a village. Therefore, there's little need for verbal communication. Each person assumes what someone else will probably say and do.

They communicate by what someone is *doing* or where *they are* physically.

> *You know how it is, you'll be somewhere, maybe polishing your riding boots. Someone walks up to you and asks, "What're you doing?" I always say "Skiing on Mt. Parnassus." What I'm **doing** should be obvious.*

In China, they'd figure out you were polishing your riding boots without asking.

In village life, cooperation is essential, they operate in "teams" - help each other. They think in terms of "we"; the concept of "I" is unknown. To think of one's self as, "I," is selfish, unacceptable - they're a community.

For an American, this perception of self is incomprehensible. I thought I'd trick one of my Chinese students into realizing that not having a concept of "I" is impossible. So, very cleverly, I put this question to him:

"How do you say 'I'm hungry?'"

My thinking is that "I" am hungry and no one else!

My student thought a moment, I suppose to translate the idea, then he said,

"The stomach needs food."

They really have no concept of "I"! But I rather imagine in America, that will change!

As a college Instructor, I had to watch some students carefully during tests as they "help" each other, share information. In America this "sharing" is not acceptable, and then when I address the issue to remove any "sharing" material, here come the water works! I have been amazed, impressed, astounded at how easily the tears flow, copiously, noisily - off - on, like a faucet! It's a gift.

This "helping," sharing information, is not limited to communal societies, but possibly there it's expected and accepted. Americans, as individuals, cheat on occasion, blatantly cheat - not "sharing," and are aggressive in their defense - no tears, but an expression of outrage for being caught! Disappointing.

Circular communication

In general, the Asians don't respond directly to questions. They smile, which is confusing to a Westerner, specifically Americans. We need words.

This is "circular" communication; it's left up to the listener to decide what is meant - not a good idea. Americans have choices of answers - there is not a single answer to any question - we have many choices of responses. We can use words, gestures, silence, make faces, hand/arm movements. Basically we depend on words.

Circular communication is commonly also "said" in metaphors. You have to listen, then see where you fit in the story. It could take awhile.

Asians also speak in metaphors; they give stories, illustrated examples instead of direct explanation - cause and effect, as

41

Americans do. We think in a straight line: If you do this, that will be the result.

Asians probably will not give you a direct, "Yes," or "No," answer. They'll give you a story (a metaphor):

> *There was a boy who lived high up in the mountains in a very small house. He had no other children around to play with so he was very lonely. Every day he would go out to take care of the goats, and, as he walked on the mountain sides, he would see in the distance a house with golden windows. He would think, "Those people in the house with the golden windows must be very happy. I wish I could go there and be with them." Then, one day, when he was older, he put on his hat, his big boots and took his staff to go to the house with the golden windows. All the day, he climbed over big rocks, crawling around big trees and thick brush. He was very tired by the end of the day. Finally, he arrived at the house with the golden windows! But, they weren't gold at all! They were just ordinary windows! He turned and looked in the distance toward his own house, and there it was, with golden windows! In the morning and evening the sun shone on the window glass and reflected the gold of the sunrise and sunset. All that he wanted he already had. He returned home and was a happy man ever after.*

And then you decide what the answer is to your question by the message of the metaphor.

AMERICAN Communication (blah, blah, blah, blah ......)

America, too, is made up, in part, of "villages." The older, established states, such as the Northeast, Mid-west and deep

South, are made up of a collection of small towns where everyone knows everyone - for generations.

They've known the families of each neighbor for almost as long as the state is old. Vermont, for example, is particularly laconic - meaning they don't verbally communicate by words if they can possibly avoid it. The main word that signifies a verbal exchange is, "A-yuh."

Yes, seriously, "A-yuh." (= yes, ok, all right, sure, uh huh, OMG!, oh…)

> *I had a close friend, Jim, in California and I told him I was taking a trip East and would go through Vermont.*
>
> *He asked me to stop by and say "Hello" to his brother at the general store where he worked (I've forgotten the town). He hadn't heard from his brother in years. I arrived at the town, went to the general store and met the brother. "Hi," I said, exuberantly. "I'm a friend of your brother, Jim. He said to stop by and say, 'Hi!'. "Without looking up, from his task, Jim's brother said, "A-yuh."*
>
> *End of visit.*

I can't resist telling you this anecdote about Vermont from some magazine. I don't recall the origin so I can't give the writer credit. I apologize.

> *A young woman walked into an antique store in Vermont. She walked over to a butter churner and asked the proprietor, "What is that?"*
>
> *"A butter churner." he replied. "I'll take that." She said. "What do you plan to do with it?" He asked. "My fiancé and I are both very shy and we have nothing to talk about.*

When he comes to visit next, he'll ask me, 'What is that?' and I'll say, 'It's a butter churner.'"

ASIAN and AMERICAN understanding of volume in communication.

In general the Asian use of "volume" in communication is 180 degrees off from the West.

The Japanese, Filipinos, posh British and others speak in a relatively low volume speech communication mode. The Japanese, in particular, are very polite to each other and there is a strong tradition of courtesy, so there's no need to speak loudly.

American Indians, in general, fit into the quieter communication group as they are communal and close knit, there's no need for volume.

Americans, Koreans, Jews, and Russians usually use considerably more volume than some Asians, in general. The Europeans vary as to what amount of volume is normal in their communication. Southern Italians are usually physically expressive. Northern Italians consider themselves elite and may be more vocally subdued.

Mother and I, both being raised as Southern Italians, were vocally expressive, apparently at some volume. This was our norm. Once, when I was about 11 years old, Mother and I were talking while one of my school friends stood by listening. When we left, my friend asked me, "Why were you yelling at your mother?"

That came as a big surprise to me.

A friend and I were strolling the streets of posh Sausalito, where we stopped at a shop of exquisite china. I was captivated by a set of delicate, exotic, pricey dinner-ware and went inside to see if I could possibly buy just a cup and saucer. Jean, my friend from Texas, was a soft-spoken woman who decided to wait outside the shop and watch the sleek sailboats on the glassy Bay.

The shop owner, a Russian woman, explained, at full volume and passion, she could not break up a set, did I know how hard it was to get those dishes, did I understand how much they were...!! Of course, I did, and we "discussed" their beauty and delicacy and I left. Jean asked me, "Why did you get that lady mad at you - I could hear her yelling clear out here?!!" "Mad?" I was confused. We always talked like that at home, but "home" was with southern Italians, not laconic Texans.

Now, when I say that certain cultures use "more volume," are "more expressive," "polite," and other adjectives, please note, these comments, observations and verbal reports are what I have noted and experienced, and what other persons, citizens of these countries have told me are their norm.

FILIPINOS and SOUTHERN AMERICANS usually speak in a softer volume.

My impression and experience with Filipinos is that they are a warm, happy people with a tendency toward being calm and mild. They don't seem ready or willing to be engaged in a loud verbal exchange.

It's the same with Americans from the deep South. They tend to be slower moving, soft spoken and courteous people. When I'm around them I have to be aware of my manners and do my best to be polite.

"It ain't necessarily so..."

Often the American knee jerk response to "generalizations" is, "not necessarily so," "not *all* Laplanders…" are trite, obvious and so banal, I'll spare you from being lumbered with them. That should be obvious.

ASIAN TIME is infinite (Chinese, Japanese, Bali, islands…)

Americans want an immediate, decisive answer to all questions. Guesswork takes time and we can't "waste" that time to guess meanings or play games with ideas.

Chinese, Asians, in general, have time. They have thousands of years to think something over. You just can't push them into a decision. Ask an Asian question and he may stand there, thinking, and never respond. Ramifications are carefully considered before making a commitment.

My last Master's Thesis included a section on the Asian use of time. That is quite literal - *they use the time, time does not control them.*

It is common for Asian students to make straight A's. Assuming intelligence is equal among students, but Asians have a higher incidence of A's, then the question is, "Why? Why do Asians get higher grade scores than other cultures?"

For one thing - they study. But, study takes time, Asians take that time, use that time. Americans have "pieces of time" - pieces never big enough to do what they have lined up for the day - all the activities on their "list".

Americans see time horizontally, Asians see it circular - it never ends.

One of my friends has been trying to broker a deal with with the Chinese for a monopoly to ship wine from China to California. The two sides have been haggling over 15 years! No end in sight. I predict a dull future for the enterprise.

American time is allotted in horizontal sections: 7:15 get up out of bed. 7:20 shower. 7:35 dress, have breakfast. 7:55 leave for school. 8:20 at school, look for a parking spot. 9:00 Anthropology class. 9:50 head for Physics class…4:05 go to library to study. Leave at 5:10 grab a McDonald's burger, head for work until 9:20, go home study until 11:14 then go to bed.

Not much time for school work.

I asked my Asian students how much time they studied. They looked at me blankly - time?

It turns out, that's what they do - study - no work, no "grab a bite" - all the periphery tasks are done for them by their parents. The student's only task is to do well in school. And, some of my students have told me that if they don't get A's, there can be serious consequences.

One Asian boy was imploring me to tell him what grade he'd get in the course.

I told him I couldn't state that yet - he'd have to wait for the Final.

He begged; I could see he was serious. He said, "If I don't get an A, my father will beat me."

I told him, "You'll get an A." I knew he was telling me the truth - he was a great kid and a very good student.

Another Asian student said, "I hate Americans! You always think we Asians make A's; so we have to make 'A's' because you think we do!"

I carefully explained to him, "We Americans expect you to make 'A's' because you always do."

It was a catch 22.

However, one critical, HUGE difference in a student's time is that Americans usually hold down a part-time job to help cover expenses. An Asian's parents support their child all through school. Not having to work, is basic for enough time to study and make decent grades.

The Need to Save face

One pervasive characteristic of most Asians, is their need to "save face". They seek to avoid negative public attention at all costs, and joking about any foibles they have is not acceptable. In general, they don't laugh easily and rarely at themselves.

You may have noticed, when there is a disaster (earthquake, fire, accident) and there is a food line or line for assistance, Asians don't crowd or shove each other; they're orderly and patient - actually to the point of being courteous.

I have always found that extraordinary.

An American man, who is familiar with Mandarin, said the Asians don't panic as a rule because they have a word in their language that says, "I'm panicking, I'm hysterical!" So, if they say that word, that's enough to explain how they feel - they don't need to "panic" as Americans would recognize that as being "normal."

I was tutoring a young Chinese man in literature. He was to interpret a passage in an essay. The passage started out similar to:

> *The young girl sat on the couch by her window watching the hard rain pour down. She sighed.*

I asked him, "How does the girl feel?"

He thought about it for awhile and said, "I have no idea what you're talking about."

He left. Perhaps there's no word for "sigh" in his language.

Two young Chinese sisters in another class were reading poetry. I told one of them, "Read this part, feel angry." Blank look. No response.

I told the other sister, "Well, you read this passage, and be angry." Blank look.

I asked them both, astonished, "Haven't you ever been angry?"

Blank looks on both; they shook their heads "No," completely baffled.

I'd like to know how to do that - Italians do anger very well.

Another Asian student, a young man, was doing exceptionally well. I said, "You're such a good student in every way. I'm very proud of you."

He stood thoughtfully for a moment and then asked, "Is it ok to tell someone they're doing good while they're still alive?"

That question took a moment to sink in. I simply replied, "Ah, yes."

Think about the implication behind that question. Pressure, stress, saving face, tradition, family pride…

Money

It might seem odd to talk about "money" as a cultural perception; but, let's face it, everywhere, "money" in some form, makes the world go 'round.

Whether we see money as clam shells, sheep skins, cattle, greenbacks or gold coins… it's a determining factor in how that society functions. And, of course, the attitude and acquisition of money rests largely on an individual's perception of self - "If I'm rich I'm great; I have value."

My mother used to say. "If you don't have a dime, not even a dog'll bark at you."

But, there are cultural attitudes about wealth developed over eons. Many countries have come to understand that "money" is handy in an exchange of goods. Money is power.

This is where the American attitude of, "You can't say that! Not all …. are …!"

Poor, deluded Americans! No, not "all … are…!" Let's just look at the *history* of attitude about money in specific areas.

Chinese

For thousands of years the Chinese have been merchants, businessmen. They're sharp in understanding human nature, what is needed, who wants what and what they're willing to pay. The Chinese have patience; they can out-wait you in making any business decisions; time is on their side.

They're shrewd, they look for a value, a good deal. They'll settle for nothing less. An exchange of value is not sufficient - they want the best possible exchange for their investment.

They designed paper money for ease of exchange. Since their physical area is vast, carrying coins, goods, merchandise and art work was cumbersome in itself and having various types of monetary exchanges was annoying and confusing. So paper money was the solution for travel.

Read the history of China, understand their brilliance, artistry and social construction. They are an amazing group of people.

Scots

Scotsmen have long been considered the "cheapest" people when it comes to spending money.

Not so.

Scots are clever, understand value for value, but will listen and bargain. They are good businessmen, trustworthy, they keep their word and give quality for quality. They are witty, open and very sharp.

GERMANS, ENGLISH

These two cultures are closely aligned. Over history there has been much interaction and alliance between the two. Both cultures are strong-willed and clever.

Their attitude toward money is identical. They don't bargain. They see an article in question as being of a certain worth in exchange, and that's it. Bargaining is not their strong suite - nor do they have any interest in it! Take it or leave it.

51

Generally in commerce or local bartering, they don't... they see a finite amount of value, and that's it. They are very open about this and they understand a business deal as finite. No returns, a bargain is a bargain.

MID EAST

"Clever" is the one word, for me, that best describes the people of the mideast. And yes, that takes in a LOT of people! Please, Americans, don't sputter and shake your head in amazement and say, "You can't include *all* people in the mideast under one label!"

Yes, I can. *It's obvious!* The life styles of the people are similar; the terrain in the mideast is similar, the ages of the civilizations are similar, their belief systems are similar... the people share many customs, needs and survival strategies.

Their attitude toward a medium of exchange is to get the most for what they sell and pay the least for what they get. Of course. But the attitude is one of life or death - survival is the goal.

Yes, the bargaining is intense - they mean business. Value for value is intense. In business, the Mid East people are low on humor, high on acumen. In their home life, they are gentle, sharing and warm people.

As an aside, I found out the reason why Arabs and other mideast people wear dark glasses, it's not for shade from the blazing desert sun; it's because when you get excited about a bargain, your eyes dilate and then the cost goes up. The merchants read how far open the pupils in your eyes dilate and they know how much to increase the price!

In business when a customer gets interested over a sale, the pupils of his eyes open wide and the seller then increases the price! If the seller can't see the amount of dilation, the price is lower. You can't see pupils through dark lenses.

When I went shopping in Turkey and Egypt the merchants saw me coming from some distance! I loved everything, and that's what they sold me - everything! And, I am so glad! Even now, I have a tapestry of camels and pyramids on my office wall. Every time I look at it, I feel the happiness of that day I bought it.

AMERICAN "THINGS"

Americans value "things," the more "things" we have the happier we are. Money is a "thing." The more money we have, the more value we have - as a person.

We don't save money - we invest it. When we buy something it's to make us look successful - valued. We prefer things to be "big," that way they have more value - "I" have more value. "Big" is good. "Bigger" is better.

We tend to trust people, think everyone means well, try to help, be of service. As Christians, usually, we believe "…freely open your hand and give him what he needs…" No, it doesn't work that way anymore.

Today people have it all figured out how to get something for nothing and whine if it's not enough. And, we Americans, apologize for our largesse.

Pathetic.

My mother used to say I spend money like a drunken sailor. Well, isn't that what it's for? What good is it in a box? I tried saving silver dollars, thinking, "Someday these'll be worth thousands!"

They weren't.

So much for capitalism.

Japanese

With the Japanese, honor, above all things, is treasured. Saving face is critical, self, pride, national pride, all taken very seriously.

Before the next anecdote, I have to tell you about myself and my life in Hawaii.

> *The state of Hawaii is governed almost entirely by Japanese influence. And, at that time I was not aware of how seriously they look at honor. Also, if you are not familiar with the world of opera, you need to know the various divisions of artists and our vanity. I am a lyric soprano which means I have a great deal of vocal range and some latitude in my repertoire. As far as rank goes, we are just below the reigning queens who are the coloraturas.*
>
> *And truly, they are the reigning class in every way. But we are both testy and vane - so be it. I owned a home on the beach at Lanikai, Oahu which I put up for sale. The Federal Administration refused to let me sell it saying it needed major repairs. I phoned them and exploded - "I bought the house this way and I intend to sell it this way!" To discuss the problem I went to the Federal Building where a Japanese official waited in the lobby crowded with mostly Japanese, people coming, going, in, out, elevators buzzing...*
>
> *My Italian soprano indignation took over. I lit into him over his refusal to sell my home. I yelled, shouted, demanded...all the while he was backing up from me. He finally backed into the elevator, the doors closed - he was gone.*

I sold the house. But I finally realized his strategy to shut me down - he thought since we were in public, I would be too shamed for a confrontation and back down.

That will never happen!

But perhaps the true nature of the Japanese people is evident after the meltdown of the Fukushima Daiichi Nuclear Power plant in 2011. Their behavior in that crisis is a perfect example of Japanese "honor."

An earthquake in that area, caused the nightmare of a devastating tsunami which resulted in the loss of 25,000 - *twenty five thousand* people, who died tragically along with their homes and all their belongings.

The people who were left behind lost everything, their homes, their families, all the things that make up a lifetime in those 2 hours of horror, no food available, no fresh water, their lives turned upside down.

The Japanese formed a line, a long line of people, waiting for food, water and what help was available. No shoving, no complaining, no impatience - just a very long line of distressed people patiently waiting for help.

Their demonstration of "honor" was an inspiration to the world. They lived "honor," their restraint, patience and inner strength in the face of disaster was a dramatic lesson of honor, of civilization to the rest of the world.

We are not all the same!

As I mentioned earlier, if you're serious about an exchange of value for value, then get an air-tight contract. Americans, please, do not be deluded into thinking a man's word is good enough - it's not!

Our innocence in business is embarrassing - too often we are sitting ducks for getting cheated. Today, a hand shake is exactly that - a hand shake! It's not a binding contract or an understanding. In a hand shake today, one side is saying to himself, "Well, I pulled that off - this fool will never figure out what hit him!"

We tend to be trusting until we realize how we've been taken, then it's too late and we sue or we come out with both guns blazing. Then our business sense is on overkill. It might be good to follow the Asian strategy of thinking ahead, carefully, for any possible pitfalls.

AMERICAN TIME

Since TIME is critical in America, we have an unwritten universal law:

"You MUST be on time."

Not early, not late - *on time.*

American rules can fluctuate a tiny bit. You may be as much as 10 (ten) minutes early, or 10 (ten) minutes late. If you more than 10 minutes early, either wait in your car, or phone the appointment and get permission to enter early (seriously!)

If you are going to be more than 10 minutes late, phone the hostess and advise her. Tell her *exactly* what time you'll be there, or estimate the best you can.

If you've had unexpected guests show up, phone the hostess, explain. Ask if they can be included; if not, then do what you have to do. It's up to your hostess to accept people in her home or not.

> *One of my closest friends I've had for years, wants guests to arrive exactly on the appointed hour. We had a luncheon date at 1:00 p.m. I happened to be 1 block from her house on that day, 15 minutes to 1:00. I phoned, "Jan, I'm in your neighborhood, can I come over now?" She was distressed. "Oh, no… I'm not ready…no…I'm busy…" So I said, "OK. I'll drive round 15 minutes." She was relieved. I arrived 15 minutes later.*

NEVER show up as a guest with other friends whom the hostess has not invited and is not expecting.

CULTURAL CONCEPTS OF TIME

There are cultures in America which usually arrive late to any function. And, when I say, "**LATE**," the word is in capital letters, flashing rays of irate red.

1. Black Americans (in general)

2. White Americans (at times)

3. Hispanics (usually)

4. Islanders (usually)

5. Native Americans (usually)

6. Very rich people (always)

7. Very poor people (always)

And, in spite of other people protesting, "You can't say that!! You can't generalize!" It's tedious!

Yes, I can. Cultures have norms - that's what makes them *"cultures."*

It drives me nuts to be kept waiting. If there's a problem, I understand. But too many people disregard your schedule and do "what feels good" to them. In main-stream America, this is unacceptable.

It's rude.

However, if you're attending an ethnic gathering, "When in Rome, do as the Romans do."

I was invited to the wedding of a Black couple. The wedding time was set for 2:00 p.m. Saturday. I showed up at 1:45 p.m. and sat down in a pew. The church was empty. I sat there for awhile wondering what happened, checked my watch, checked the invitation...? Right day. Right time.

Right church.

About 2:30 four men walked in hauling sound equipment - they looked at me, confused. I looked at them, confused. They started to set up the sound equipment, talking about what to do, where to set what...I left.

American Indians We call them Native Americans now...why? Who is this "we"...? Me? No, not **me** and not most of the American Indians I know. That population is indifferent as to what labels others use. Some Indians are, Hopi, Cherokee, Navaho, Sioux, Apache, Black Foot, Plains, Osage, Arapaho...

Who was the ill-informed speech dictator who decided to change the reference of that population? Who set himself up to understand the needs of an indigenous population and change their identity- to "thee" Native American? A one-size fits all?

Did anyone take their vote on "who-to-be"?

Someone quite arrogant, quite ignorant. I sincerely doubt that it was an American Indian who decided to obliterate his heritage.

One of my fellow Instructors in college was teaching a class about "thee" Native Americans. She was explaining how "thee" Native American observes "their" death ritual. It seems "thee" Native American lies his dead relatives on tall biers made of dry stalks and then burns the bodies.

That's a big part of the problem - there's no single kind of American Indian. We have a huge group of disparate peoples who have different customs, language, government, and, identities.

When "The Europeans" (undocumented immigrants) first landed at Plymouth Rock, there were 22,000 separate tribes of natives. Some of them shared a language, but most had their own language and culture.

Some tribes were "healers" - they were sort of EMT's for other tribes and were not nomads or warriors. They created herbal remedies and were patronized by other tribes for healing.

Some tribes migrated; they followed the herds of wild animals for food - buffalo, for example. Other tribes migrated by season to follow the fruit and grains naturally grown by nature - organic!

There were tribes that farmed, didn't migrate. They built "homes," community centers; they had a physically stable culture.

Some tribes were "sportsmen" - they had slaves and used people for target practice.

Anyone born in America is a "native" American. If you insist on differentiating "natives," perhaps call the tribe in question by its correct tribal name: Navajo, Apache, Arapaho, Seminole, Sioux, Osage...

Ohhh...it's odd that the Osage tribe comes up. Have any of you heard of the Osage? Probably not. Well, I'm part Osage; at present they're located in northern Oklahoma. The sun was their father and the moon their mother, they are, "Children of the middle waters."

They lived as warriors, fearless warriors. In combat the point was to kill the opposition; they took no prisoners. The Osage had no fear of death - if you get killed, hey! that's the name of the game!

According to history, every tribe feared them - especially the Cherokees. The ferocity of the Osage was unparalleled. If they wanted supplies, a wagon train for example, they killed the supplier and helped themselves. It was expedient for the Osage, but distressful for the army which relied on wagon-train supplies.

> *One occasion I had charge of a young lady from France who I was to take on a tour of the San Francisco Bay Peninsula. She spoke some English and I spoke some French so we did quite well together. I took her to the City (San Francisco), then to the Mission of Our Lady of Carmel, down the beautiful west coast. We stopped at the major points of interest. After three days she was to leave. She said how much she enjoyed the trip, but that she wished she could meet a Native American.*

> *I laughed and said, "You've been sitting next to one for three days!" She didn't believe me. What was she expecting? A headband with a feather?*

Also, some American Indians do not laugh easily as many Europeans do. I can hear or see something that I think is hilarious and not crack a smile. The Indian gets the joke, but doesn't laugh out loud. Laughter, humor, is cultural.

(Even though I was raised deep into Italian culture, I find Italian humor to be buffo - not my style. I prefer the understated British humor where you're mind fills in the funny stuff - you're on your own there!)

Years ago Bert Lahr, an American comedian, put on a comedy show in Alaska for Eskimos. After 2 hours knocking himself out with schtick, no one laughed. He thought he bombed; no, it was the Eskimos' way of enjoying themselves - they didn't laugh - they didn't leave. He was great!

Each tribe has its own system of law, of family interaction, own kind of religion, architecture, art work. Also, over the years and trips to cultural centers, I've found that some American Indian and Chinese art is identical - fascinating.

There's the Chinese, "Hopei," similar to "Hopi." The Chinese "Kansu," similar to "Kansas." The designs on the woven baskets are similar. In my mind, this "similarity" is beyond coincidence.

Some American Indian tribes operate under a female rule, some prefer male rule.

Respect their cultures, do not lump them together as Americans have been incorrectly trained, "'Thee' Native Americans…" grossly inaccurate. That reference assumes there is only one tribe.

> *As a complete aside: I had a private student who was a paleontologist. There is a wide-spread theory by anthropologists and cultural scientists, that the Chinese migrated to North America and became our Indians. My student said, the American Indians migrated west and became Chinese. He presented a paper on it, but I never heard results. To me, they could have migrated both ways - at this point in time who can "prove" what? And, does it really make any difference?*

Communication Style of American Indians

In general, they're taciturn, rarely talk, do a great deal of observation. When they do communicate verbally it's "circular" -

by metaphors, never a direct answer. You have to "guess" what they mean; you have to make those dangerous assumptions that mainstream Americans try conscientiously to avoid.

My Italian peasant mother and Osage father communicated in circular terms. Drove me nuts. I never knew what they wanted and they were upset with me for not cooperating. They never got to the point. I was always left guessing - and those guesses covered a lot of territory - I always wrong; they were always annoyed.

Japanese, Korean, Taiwanese, and other Asians

Are all similar in their use of time; time is used as needed - it does not get priority. They have low verbal communication, with a high context reliance on visual communication. They are traditional, family oriented and high scholastic achievement.

Indian (East) language and customs

In Silicon Valley these people are referred to as "dot" Indians as some Indians - Hindus in particular, often have a red dot in the center of their forehead. This red dot is called a "bindi". It's a symbol, a reminder of the third eye in meditation. The third eye is connected to the Absolute and is to remind you of your immortality, your connection to God.

In my experience as instructor of mideast people, in general, they're *extremely* intelligent.When I first interacted with Asian students and a mideast student responded accurately to my questions, I was impressed. The concepts I teach are often obtuse, obscure and complex and these students understood the concepts well.

They also communicate in circular form - you have to guess what they mean. That can be very annoying to a mainstream American

- say what's on your mind! We don't have time to play games, to guess what you mean!

For a student to grasp their import the first time around is astounding!

Surely, one or two students of a specific group in a class would be exceptionally intelligent. But for the mideast students, in my classes, it was the norm.

In their own culture time is not an issue; they do what they have to do and then move on. Time does not limit their business at hand. However, when merging with American mainstream they'll easily adjust to our custom and be on time.

Russians

This is another group of extremely intelligent people - they have to be to speak Russian! They have a great sense of humor and they try to fit in. They consider themselves "Western" as far as culture goes; they assimilate easily.

Their priorities are higher education, family and good neighbors. Like us, they're not necessarily communal, but are often individuals, creative achievers.

They understand direct communication, verbal exchange is easy and metaphors are readily understood.

Vietnamese

They're fast-learners, achievers and warm-hearted. From hearing their stories of starvation and the horror of war, they tell how grateful they are to be in America. I had one student who worked full time and paid what bills he had to, then sent the rest of his money to Viet Nam to fight Communists.

He helped pay for an underground newspaper that carried news from the outside world and gave ways to escape from that area. Their dedication to American is impressive and sincere.

There is no problem in communication with them. They want very much to assimilate and be upstanding citizens.

Filipinos

I think, more than any other group, they love children, and seem to be, in general warm, intelligent, cooperative people. They are communal, family comes first. They appreciate the American concern for time and are very reliable when meeting a schedule.

Also, although I run the risk of generalizing here, I tend to find them to be very musical. Music flows out of them, song, dance, gracefulness. They are a joy to watch at their festivals; they have a spirit of Life that's contagious.

Mexican-Americans

Another communal group. Mexican Americans are family oriented - family comes first. Time for them is not an issue, it has low value; they approach time as just a part of the day, not an entity in itself.

Communication is usually open and easy. My Mexican American students have told me that there are various traditions among them; according to the state, or area you're from in Mexico, the traditions and social expectation; they are not all "Mexicans" as Americans tend to lump them.

In one tradition, if they meet an "American" friend in public, they won't speak to that person - the Mexican Americans "don't see" the American. I couldn't find out why this was a social custom.

But, other Mexican-Americans have no problem saying,"Hello," to an American friend in public - oh, by the way, the Mexicans refer to Americans as "English" people. I find that amusing and I wonder how the "English" feel about that!

Being that they are communal, they do not differentiate between "yours" and "mine" as far as property goes. If they need something, they use it, take it. For them it's a convenience. They approach someone's belongings as "ours," not "mine." Often they refer to each other as "cousin," extended families.

In mainstream America, where individuals reside, a communal approach to personal property is not tolerated. There are many misunderstandings.

In some of my other books, I've spoken at length about calling Mexican Americans "Hispanic". They are not "Hispanic" any more than Americans are "Anglo's"- it's ludicrous! If they're born in Mexico and become citizens here, they're Mexican Americans. But anyone born here is just plain old American.

One problem for Americans (or, anyone else!) is when working with a communal society is their habit of functioning as a group.

*I had organized a pot-luck dinner at my church. I knew a Mexican-American woman with three children, all of whom danced Folklorico. So, I asked her and her three children (the FOUR of them) to come to my church at 6:00pm, have dinner, and **after dinner**, at 7:00 pm the children could dance for entertainment, and I'd pay them. 6:00pm came and went. 6:15, 6:30, 6:45, still no dancers. Then, at 7:00 pm here she comes, her with her 3 children, her boyfriend, his best friend, his best friend's girl friend and her 3 children. SIX extra people, unannounced, uninvited. I about fell over. The food was all gone. The*

*woman shot me a look of disgust. Her children danced, I
paid them and they left - annoyed.*

I thought, the next time I invite someone out of mainstream
America, I'll stipulate the ground rules so we're all on the same
page. Had I known she was coming with an entourage, I would
have prepared enough food for them to enjoy. But, it's *rude* to
show up anywhere if you're not *specifically* invited, and
especially *en masse.*

Black Americans

There are numerous social customs of Blacks. Generally they are
high verbal, expressive, warm natured and generous.

For many Black Americans, time is not a part of their culture -
they move according to what they plan for that day and focus on
the occasion itself. Plans could change momentarily. When you
go to a Black function, plan to stay awhile, relax, enjoy, as the
function could take place at any hour and last to any hour.

Being causal about time restrictions and limitations can cause
misunderstandings and friction in Mainstream society. One of my
friends was an opera singer, a tenor, lead singer, gorgeous voice!
And he usually showed up late for rehearsals - VERY LATE.

Not good.

Even though his talent was prized he was not invited back for
performances - which he attributed to racism. I firmly assured
him it was not a race issue - it was one of *promptness for all*
opera members. He was not convinced.

In general Blacks are communal, "brothers" and "sisters," an
extended family. Similar to Mexican Americans, they support

each other as the need requires. If you invite a Black friend to dinner, plan on a group showing up - unless you specify.

There is little concept of "mine" - it's "ours". In general, property is "ours" and used as needed. An individual's belongings are not solely his or hers, but belongs to the community - usually.

In mainstream America this habit of "borrowing" property is often misunderstood and results in serious ramifications.

Mainstream Americans see property as "mine," or "yours." Keep away from "mine" and I'll ask permission to "borrow" yours. I do not intend to keep it. And, whatever the article is, it must be returned, promptly, in the same condition it was borrowed. If it is lost or damaged, it must be replaced.

I have purposely not referred to Blacks as "African Americans". Saying "African" American is the same as saying we are North Americans. We are; but that's HUGE piece of real estate - exactly what part of North America are you from? Canada? Mexico? North Pole? Alabama? Each area has a different culture from its neighbors, and each is protective of its identity.

So it is with Africa. Each area, each *country*, may have a vastly different culture from its neighbors. And, what arrogance of Americans to lump them all together! I have been to "Africa" (Egypt) and they do not refer to themselves as a "lumped" country - *they are Egyptians - not "Africans."*

I have had students from Kenya, Republic of the Congo (which they refer to simply as "Congo"), Botswana, Ethiopia, Eritrea… with their stories of their country, the various foods, customs, dances and attractions. They are each immensely proud of their country - as they should be. But, *they do not call themselves "Africans."*

Islanders

Yes, any island - all islands. To live on an island - we should all be so lucky. What more is there to say? There's a relaxed, casual sort of careless approach to time, communication and appointments.

One of my students was the son of an official in the Caribbean government. He was always late to class, totally indifferent to the rules, ignored the requirements of the class syllabus, handed in - or not - required data, was pretty much indifferent to the entire time structure of the school.

He was giving a presentation and was running considerably over the time limit.

I told him he'd have to sit down - it was someone else' time slot. Annoyed he stated he wasn't done yet; he'd sit when he was done. He faced me during the time he chastised me, looked down on me, and "put me in my place."

Oh, sez I, but you *are* done and smiled benignly. Still annoyed, he sez if you don't give me an A in this class I'll drop it.

I sez, rather amused, do what you want; I am not guaranteeing you an A. He dropped the class.

Alas...America is not an island! The young man has a steep learning curve.

Tonga

Several times I have had Tongan's in my classes. There are communal, very family oriented. They are also out-going, musical and just plain fun. They bring their native foods to share, they do their custom dances and explain the movements to the class. They also explain the cultural make-up of who behaves in what way. They are deeply religious, as a rule, and the girls are virgins until they marry.

This sounds like a design for a very successful community!

Mainstream Americans - "Lumping" Cultures - "Double-think" - generalizing.

Many Americans - those who don't travel or read history, will be indignant at the thought of "most" of the (insert specific group name here) will always be late or "help" each other at tests, or are inherently musical.

These Americans will say, "You can't say that! All ..... (insert name here) don't do that! People are individuals! You can't generalize! You have to take one individual at a time!"

Well, there is a huge problem with that kind of thinking.

It's not true. Not all cultures are individualistic - that's generalizing.

The same people who whine "You can't generalize!" are the same ones who say, "Republicans are *all...*," "Capitalists are *all...*" "Rich people *don't...*" - when *they* generalize - it's Truth! But, when others generalize, it's *stereotyping*! What it really is, is *tiresome*! It's a lack of logic - a lack of analyzing, critical thinking!

And, often, when *you* generalize, *they* say, "You just don't understand... you can't say that." The implication in that statement is that "we," Americans in general, do not say things like that - which is a generalization.

What someone is really saying when they tell you not to generalize is, "Don't say that - it displeases *me*!" So-o-o American!! The covert message of an American is, "When I say we need to help 'others,' I mean only the people I approve of."

Groups of people do have similar characteristics - obviously! If you are raised in a specific group that demonstrates specific characteristics, more likely than not, you will exhibit those characteristics. (I learned to talk like that in my Master's classes. We're trained to think alike. - oops, that's a stereotype!)

THE AMERICAN WAY OF LIFE

This section is for immigrants, foreigners, newcomers, visitors, and anyone who drops by.

American Double-think

Americans try so hard to be all things to all people. We want so desperately for others to see us as generous, benevolent, understanding, helpful, interested, flexible, kind, humorous, intelligent, achievers, dependable…and - we are.

Note, I said *we* are. *We all* fit the above description. Whatever *we* do is the right thing to think, to say, to do - just ask us!

But…if you should happen to say *all* Italians… (insert characteristics here, good cooks, musical, handsome, healthy, etc.) Americans would be enraged - "You can't say that! Not *all* Italians are…"

We speak out of both sides of our mouth - it's "double-think."

Americans try so hard to be "fair;" so we censor opinions other than ours - which in translation, means MINE - my opinion is the right one. MY observations, habits, and perceptions are the right ones. We are encouraged to be "different" as long as you stay in the standard blue print, the proscribed boundaries of predictable, acceptable general behavior.

> *I was at a BBQ of a strong-minded, leftist neighbor. In the group of people was a woman who was a musician, a*

singer. I asked her where she sang as a rule and she mentioned a small, obscure church.

Surprised, I said, "Oh! I've sung there, too!" My neighbor, the hostess, heard me mention "church" and snarled at me, "Are you talking to someone about their religion!!"

I was completely caught off-guard. Talking about religion is verboten in homes where freedom of expression - "if it feels good, do it" - is paramount - unless, of course, the hostess is of a different belief - then, you are firmly censored. The person to whom I was speaking, hastened to explain, "She was talking about music." Appeased, that I was not crossing her boundaries of acceptable opinion, our liberal, "thought-police" hostess moved on.

You can be "different" as long as we're all the same. (I sometimes wonder what people do when they need to think *logically*? Is there an "app" for that?)

There's no cure for that lack of logic - double-think. What we really want is for everyone to feel welcome and safe. We want everyone to grow, succeed, fit in and be just like us - only different if you want, *approved* self-expression is ok. Tradition, manners, universal respect are verboten today - uh, not necessarily...

RACISM

The concept of "racism" is warped, distorted and bandied around, used as a bolt of lightening in the heart of any situation where someone is unhappy with someone else' point of view.

It means *nothing*. ***NOTHING!***

And yet, it is one of the favorite, handy slurs thoughtlessly used to accuse someone of disagreeing with your point of view - they're accusing you of what they are!

In the Trump/Hilary Presidential contest the words, "racist" and "bigot," were slung at people like offal cannon balls.

In one of my Communication classes my students were having a heated discussion about candidates who were perceived as "racist." In listening to the pointless argument, I was gritting my teeth.

The stupidity and vacuous use of the words was extremely offensive to me. I don't mind what words someone uses as long as they're appropriate and correctly used.

I interrupted the discussion to ask for a definition of the terminology they used.

Blank faces.

I explained, "It seems to me that if you're going to label people with offensive words, you should know what those words mean."

They were clueless. For me, a display of abject ignorance.

The concepts of, "race" and "bigot" are closely related. The concept, "Race" designates body structure and skin color. There are bodies that are created in specific ways for survival for a specific group of people in a specific area - as I understand the current scientific lore.

Not all bodies were created equally.

As to "why" we're created in different style bodies is an idea beyond my comprehension. For that question you need to address someone far more Intelligent than I.

The word, "racist," means either to prefer one race over another - you perceive one specific race to be superior, or, you see the same specific race to be inferior.

"Racism" is a totally negative, or, totally positive attitude toward one race. The word is meaningless; it cancels itself out. "bigot" is the same - meaningless.

Don't bother to use these words - they are not intelligent.

(And for your basic info, Google isn't always accurate - it makes many mistakes. So take what it says with a lot of room - a lotta salt.)

AMERICAN ABSOLUTES (In General)

I am defining Americans as those who have at least a high school education, a job, home, family, married, 2 - 3 children, mortgage, credit card maxed out, probably Christians and have in-laws. They will have no second language, but they can say, "Hello, my name is John," in Spanish - even if their name is really "Algernon."

We are territorial.

We *own* our things: Dogs, car, yard, tools, computer…I paid for it - it's mine, *keep your hands off!*

Most of us have a fence around our property designating boundaries - this is *my* side, that's *your* side; stay over there. Don't touch my stuff.

If you need to use something of mine, you ask me if it's ok - you don't take it without asking first. You return it the same way you got it. If you break it or lose it, you pay me for it.

I will respect your property the same way.

Be on time

There is nothing that distresses an American more than having to wait for an appointment or a person - or a red light. Time is always an issue; we never have enough or, we have time on our hands - what to do? We can't sit still, be quiet.

We might miss something, an opportunity… who knows what?

If you have to be somewhere at a specific time and you're going to be late, phone the other person, company or appointment, tell them you're going to be late. Never be late and never show up early for an appointment unless you have asked permission to do so.

> *I went to see Dr. Berry, a renowned Stanford ENT about some vocal-chord problem I was having. My appointment was at 9:00 a.m. I arrived at 8:45 so as not to be late. 9:05, 9:10, 9:15 came and went. Dr. Berry sauntered in at 9:20, chewing gum, said "Hello," to the nurses who replied, "Good morning, Doctor." He sorted through the mail and sauntered into into the depths of a hallway. I approached the desk and said, "My appointment was at 9:00. It is now 9:45. How soon will it be convenient for Dr. to see me?" The nurse glared at me, escorted me into a small room, took away all my clothes and I sat, naked, for some time. Eventually Dr. Berry walked in, looked at me and said, "The reason you're having voice problems is because you're too fat!" and walked out. Dressed, I paid his fee and left. He was deliberately late, but the worst part of the insult is to be kept waiting.*

Keep your distance

Unlike communal societies, Americans are individualistic, keep your distance. You can get as close as 2 1/2 feet near me, but that's enough. Don't touch me. We cherish our personal space; it represents freedom.

Maintain eye contact

If we are talking, please look directly in my eyes. If we are not talking you may look directly in mu eyes after a distance of 10 feet or more. Any closer is too personal. In e at the ceiling or the changing floor numbers - fascinating!

Be fair

Americans pride ourselves in being fair. Equality is our code word, one for all, share equally all rewards.

It is quite common in competition, especially with children, to give each child a blue ribbon and be a winner! We want to play fair and have each child feel important and an achiever.

Now you, foreigners, immigrants, may find this strategy asinine, even stupid. But, as yet you do not understand how important it is to "play fair" in our world. The fact that playing down an individual's achievements may actually destroy incentive, crush creativity and stultify self-worth is not as important as teaching a child it is more important to get a prize than to be honest.

People in the Midwest go to church because they respect the Ten Commandments and get married in the church with friends and family filling the pews. Everyone is happy for them.

They often have 3, 4, 5 children and two dogs, maybe a cat. Dogs and boys are considered essentials in an American family. It is expected every family will have at least one of each. The dogs will not be thoroughbreds; they'll be from a friend's litter of pups and have names like Buddy and Spot.

They are friendly, honest, hardworking people who get along with their neighbors and vote. They have BBQ's often and have several friends who talk politics and farm stuff, but mostly sports, football, baseball and some basketball. The women will join in as much as the men.

And, we Americans are very fair - unless there is someone better than you, someone we prefer to win, someone we especially like or have been paid to promote. Particularly in religions, where members of the same religious organization are greeted with a secret handshake so they are promoted ahead of others in the work-force, hired ahead of others workforce, given more support than others, etc.

And, those of us who are not in that religion shut our eyes to this practice and pretend this cheating doesn't exist. That's fair. We toss our head and say, "They wouldn't do that! It's not right!"

American police

In general, we are taught to understand the police are our friends. And if you live in certain neighborhoods, the police are friendlier than in other neighborhoods. As Americans we do have rights - also with the police, lots of them and it's best to know them well - just in case.

> *I had a class of 8 Russians to whom I taught American English and American life-style. Since they were reasonably new to America they were apprehensive as to how to relate to police in general. I explained my perspective which is they'rehelpers in time of need. The students mentioned that 4 of them were in a car that was hit by an official police car with two police officers who informed the Russians that you can't sue the Police - so they all left. The Russians asked if that were correct. I was furious and explained in America we have the right to sue anyone! We have rights that apply the same to each and every person!*

In America, assuming you are a basic citizen moving and acting in a basic American manner, you have nothing to fear from the police. They have always been wonderful to me and I treat them with respect. How could you have a civilized society without them?

But people from other countries too often have a strong fear of authority imprinted in their belief system. They live looking over their shoulder in fear of some unknown, imminent punishment.

> *Judy, a Chinese friend, and I were at an up-scale bar. She was buying. I ordered a Tangueray martini with a twist. The place was crowded and the waitress brought a martini with an olive. I pointed out that this was not what I ordered. She took it and returned the drink with a twist but it was still the same martini with the taste of brine. Really, do you think someone who drinks martinis doesn't know the difference between brine and lemon peel? I stood up to return the drink and get another. Judy clutched at my arm, pulling on my sleeve, trying to drag me back into my seat. "Please, please, don't make trouble!" She begged. "What trouble?" I asked. "All I'm going to do is get the right drink." Judy was almost in tears, begging me, dragging me down, pulling on me - "don't make trouble" the mantra. She was afraid of police retaliation. Annoyed, but to please her, I sat back down and left the drink alone.*

Apparently, in China, complaints or problems with a public establishment are not allowed or expected. There must be a deep-seated fear of the police.

The Midwest

This is the area that epitomizes the American's concept of America. The major holidays are: 4th of July, Christmas, Easter and Thanksgiving. All these mentioned are our biggest concern, our looked-forward to events.

By the way, the Midwest boundaries depend on where you live in the contiguous states. From Nebraska, sort of, over to Ohio - ish is considered Mid- west. From Kentucky south to the Florida Keys over to Louisiana is considered South.

From Colorado to Nevada is the (wild) West and from Delaware to Maine is considered North. This is all "sort of." Texas is a world in itself as is California. And, Alaska is a state - somewhere....

If you live in Massachusetts, Chicago is considered out "West." And if you live in California, Chicago is considered back "East."

But none of this really matters because Americans usually have no idea what state is next door. When I returned to the Mainland from a long stay in Hawaii, many Americans asked me if I drove home. After the fourth time of explaining, "No, I flew..." I finally just answered, "Yes. I drove." Why confuse them...?

DOWNGRADING AMERICAN ACHIEVEMENTS

It is politically and socially expedient to down-grade American accomplishments.

We don't want the world at large to think we actually work hard for what we have and any successes we have are attributed to coincidence or just luck.

An American gets an idea, goes to school, spends thousands of hours and dollars perfecting the idea, opens a business, hires hundreds of people to manufacture the idea and then he makes a very comfortable living.

And, after all the initial output, sweat and tears, the product is successful, the American sits back, counts his shekels, then some bird brain will note, "Well, you didn't do it alone."

NO ONE DOES ANYTHING ALONE! It takes us all, nose to the grindstone, early bird gets the worm, time is money, as you sow so shall you reap...need I go on? To succeed in almost any endeavor, we need others, cooperation, share in the hard parts and enjoy the good parts.

Capitalism

The brilliant Capitalist who got an idea needs help producing the idea.

The unskilled, untutored Laborer needs a steady income to depend on to provide a home for his family.

The Capitalist and the Laborer strike up a compatible arrangement and exchange commodities; the Capitalist hands over money - security, to the Laborer, and the Laborer provides his energy, strength and integrity to the Capitalist.

There is an agreeable exchange of commodities in any endeavor. And if the exchange is not acceptable, move on.

We Americans need to stop apologizing for our success. Anyone can be successful - all anyone need to do is work, work, work, try, try, again after failure - and keep on moving ahead.

As Benjamin Franklin said, "The harder I work, the luckier I get."

Imperialism

Recently I read a book written by a young American man, who was raised in a family of Socialists. He was taught to see Americans as a people who exploit "poor" countries by robbing them of their natural resources and destroying their way of life.

This altruistic young man was saturated with anti-capitalistic ideas. So he decided, on his own, he would travel to the far reaches of the earth to save the down-trodden, depressed countries that were economically raped by American capitalists and saturated with imperialistic attitudes.

So, to the end of saving the poor of the world, those natives who are exploited by greedy Capitalists, he took a semester off from Harvard (yes….HARVARD!!), started off with his designer gear slung over the back of Rosinante and headed off, alone, head held high, chin thrust nobly forward, resolute, to the wilds of Peru, where he would, single handedly, rescue the starving, naked natives from the steel grip of American imperialism.

He was disappointed in his quest.

The natives, Peruvian citizens, were quite civilized, poor - by American Standards, but not suffering from deprivation. As a nice-looking "impoverished" American male student he was welcomed into their homes, fed and helped with transportation to the various targets of his desire to change the way Peruvians lived - in other words change their way of life to what he considered better standards - *imperialism* from his standards, his point of view.

And, as a "penniless" traveler, this Harvard student managed to scarf down the peasants' food, slept in their bed, and took advantage of transportation of those downtrodden victims of capitalism. He paid for almost nothing on his trip.

This student-revolutionary explained, in his book, how he would sit at table with the natives and try to discuss imperialism, but, no one was interested. The Peruvians preferred to discuss the dull day at the office, the traffic, taxes - you know really boring stuff like the American heard at home.

So he went off to the University where the students were actually having an uprising against - you guessed it - imperialism!! At last, this leftist student, victim of capitalism and a second-hand SUV, could leap into the fray and save socialism!

The masked students were throwing stones at the militia and the militia was shooting real bullets at them. Now, I'm not a Harvard grad, but I would think it's a good idea to get the hell outta there!

It seems the protest was because the Peruvian government had some land to sell and the Americans wanted to buy it!

A simple straight-forward real estate deal!

But, no… if Americans pay for land, it must be imperialism!

And, what did our benevolent, socialist Harvard student give to the downtrodden Peruvians…?

Nothing.

Almost any other country (except Australia) is thousands of years older than America. We are 400 years old, and, the most powerful, most successful, richest, healthiest, smartest country to date. So, why are we to blame if some country, thousands of years older, lives in a tradition which could be possibly updated to provide more comfort for its people?

Why do we get blamed because other countries cling to tradition, a way of life that has not benefited its populations sufficiently?

Somewhere I read that to be successful, do what successful people do.

Outside of exporting MacDonald's, imperialism may not be such a bad idea.

HISTORY? - WHOSE?

Previously I stated Americans are abysmally ignorant of history, even our own. For a young country we do have a lot of history, but that's no excuse not to know some of it. Before we denounce ourselves as Capitalists, Imperialists, Racists, Leftists, Rightists, we need to know who we are, why we're here and how we got here.

We need to know our history.

Now the chorus cries out - "Who's history?!" Meaning "history" is recorded by the victor. The "good guys" are the ones who won the wars, by decimating the opposition, enslaving the remains of the previous population - and so on.

Yup, those are the good guys.

But what is the purpose of war? To win it? This planet has been engaged in wars since the Big Bang went off signaling the starting shot. Americans did not invent war; we just made it bigger, faster and a lot more profitable.

What is the purpose of history? To record the successes of war and minimize the methods, strategies by which wars are won. That way the Victor looks blameless - even victimized, on occasion.

Traditionally Americans, like all victors, have had our "heroes" advertised in statues, paintings and stories. We were proud of our heroes, their bravery in the face of overwhelming odds, also their combined wisdom that created a Democracy like no other.

Now, the trend of the intellects and society is to destroy the deeds and memories of some heroes of the past - the Confederates. Why? Is this not our history? At that time of our history, these Confederates were heroes. Now we realize that they, too, were victims of a time when this nation walked in ignorance.

Yes, we had slaves. Yes, the Blacks were sold by their chiefs in Africa for trinkets, chained, loaded into ships in unbelievably horrible conditions and brought to the New World, where they were sold like cattle and treated like animals for the remainder of their lives.

Now we know it was wrong, *wrong*, and we are ashamed. ***Ashamed***.

The Ugly American

But, this is our history. Yes, it's OUR history, some of it ugly. Some of it today we can't understand what great damage was done to a people. We can't live it down - we can't forget. So, why do we want to erase the ugliness of our history…? It's who we are. It's how we got where we are. And, now we have the opportunity to attempt to right a wrong, to address the damage of the past and move ahead intelligently. We stand, ashamed of our ignorance at a time when ignorance and hubris permeated all civilizations. Now, we will fix it, correct it, and all of us - together - move ahead.

On the other hand, millions of refugees came here, boatloads of immigrants, carrying their belongings in carpet bags, clutching the remnants and memories of their war- torn past to the safety of our welcoming Statue of Liberty.

Yes, we have our ugly history and our magnificent history - the history that gave the millions of poor, starving immigrants, thousands of refugees fleeing from war, oppression and pervasive fear, a chance at freedom, a good life in the New World.

The immigrants, the slaves, all the people who were the foundation of this magnificent country deserve to have their place in history. They, each one, is the foundation of who we are. There is nothing to erase, nothing to hide; the good, bad and ugly, all have their place in American history.

People still immigrate to this great country and always will. We are unique, open, welcoming. And uniquely, the door to America swings both ways. If you're happy here, fine; if you're not, its very easy to pick up your bags and step out into a better country somewhere else. You need no clearance papers to leave America.

Anti-Semitic

My family, for the most part is anti Semitic. This ignorance goes back for generations - to the old country. I think this affliction is more of a habit or tradition than it is one of experience and certainly not one of intelligence.

> *As a six year old in Worcester, Massachusetts, 1937, I was in the kitchen with mother. The "kitchen" being one room with a kerosine burner and a sink, oh yes, and an ice box. We lived in the top of a 3-story tenement looking over the tenement dumpster and car lot. It was the middle of the Depression, everyone was poor. As mother puttered at the stove, she muttered something about the Jews. On some occasions I heard various family members speaking badly of Jews and I couldn't understand why. So I asked Mother, "Who are the Jews?" Mother replied, "They're God's chosen people."*
>
> *?... God's **chosen** people...? Confused, I asked, "Well then, why aren't we Jews?" "Oh, no! No, no, no.." Was all*

I could get. The only Jews I knew of were the Hasidic Jews who wore black hats and had long side curls. They walked the city streets carrying an upside down cane with day-old bagels on it stacked high, 3 for a nickel. We often had the day-old bagels or burned toast and oatmeal for breakfast. Mother said they were good for your teeth. (To this day I have my own teeth.) Time rolled on. As to my question about Jews, I never mentioned it again. But, later in life, in my 40's, I still wanted to know who they were.

I lived in San Francisco near Brotherhood Way, a boulevard of places of worship. Temple Beth Judea was near my home so I decided to join their choir and learn about the Jews for myself. I sang with them for four years, a soloist on High Holy Days, a guest at parties, functions and celebrations. I felt very much at home. And I learned that they are a generous, kind, dedicated people, intelligent and a great sense of humor - all except Rabbi Morris who never even smiled. But the Cantor made up for him! He was so much fun!

GO THERE, LIVE AMONG THEM, BE ONE OF THEM

So, what I'm saying is, if you want to know a people, go, be with them. Live with them, eat their food, listen to their tales, laugh at their jokes, cry with their sorrows.

This is a wonderful freeing experience. You'll grow, become informed and lose fear of the unknown.

Americans who "hate" America

In every country (except maybe France) there are malcontents, people who hate their country. Probably you could put those people in Paradise and they would find something to complain about - mosquitos? Horse flies? Neighbors?

America is not perfect, I suppose - but we've all done very well here.

This cultural guide is not definitive - it couldn't be. Languages go on infinitely, affected by area, tribe, dissension, assimilation... But, humans are resilient - together we'll eventually get through any change and make it work for all.

SUGGESTED READINGS:

D'Souza, Dinesh (anything by him)

Fell, Barry Saga America (ca 1530 - 1532)

Mann, Charles C.: 1493 Discovering the New World Columbus Created

Matthews, John Joseph: Osages: Children of the Middle Waters

Menzies, Gavin: 1421 The Year China Discovered America

Nunez, Alvar Cabeza de Vaca: The Interior of America in the 1500's

ABOUT THE AUTHOR

Carolyn Franklin

Carolyn Franklin M. A. taught Communication Studies for 30 years in Los Altos, and Saratoga Colleges. She discovered rhetoric and how pervasive it is in verbal and non verbal communication, dominating the direction of all the speakers all of the time - a fascinating and handy discovery! Also, as a trained singer in the San Francisco opera chorus, her avocation is coaching speakers to have the most effective voice possible for their communication. The sound and use of the voice are primary in rhetoric! Her dogs love classical music, too, especially Strauss waltzes.

M. A. Communication Studies

M. A. Education

B. A. Psychology

30 years voice training (San Francisco Opera)

Voice/Speech improvement Coach

voicedynamicscf@yahoo.com

OTHER BOOKS BY CAROLYN FRANKLIN

Police Brutality: A solution

Adam: First man, or, first mouse?

Emotional Intelligence: Like yourself

Coping With Bullies: A gentle approach

You Can Catch More Flies With Honey: The Art Of Rhetoric, Persuasion, Manipulation, and Blarney

Your Voice – Your Personality The Total You

Women Bullying Women: An effect of Women's Lib

Rx For Your Communication Ills - The ULTIMATE Book on Communication

Women At Work: Win-Win Communication Strategies

#MeToo, NOW, Women's Lib, Just Say No: Why they won't work

Athena: Goddess of Communication Strategies

Welfare + Diversity: Social Suicide

The Story of Mary: Mayhem, mirth and miracles

The Princess And The Pee: Caring For A "Special Needs" Person

Made in the USA
Coppell, TX
10 December 2021

68003925R00056